WATERSKIING
is for me

WATERSKIING is for me

Carole S. Briggs

photographs by
Bob and Diane Wolfe

Lerner Publications Company Minneapolis

The author wishes to thank Steve Bush, Anne Marie Campbell, Wendy Campbell, Joey Benedict, Eric Bachinski, Jessamae and Tref Friedman, Orin Schlome, Kal Logelin, Peggy and Harlan Anderson, Gretchen and Jerry Wilmes, Marybeth Campbell, and Morgan Williams for their help in the preparation of this book.

Editor: Nancy M. Campbell
Editorial Consultant: Stephen Bush
Steve's Ski School
Prior Lake, Minnesota

LIBRARY OF CONGRESS CATALOGING IN PUBLICATION DATA

Briggs, Carole S.
Waterskiing is for me.

(A Sports for me book)
Summary: A girl learning to water ski describes the equipment, techniques, and safety rules of the sport.
1. Water skiing—Juvenile literature. 2. Water skiing—Safety measures—Juvenile literature. [1. Water skiing] I. Wolfe, Robert L., ill. II. Wolfe, Diane, ill. III. Title. IV. Series: Sports for me books.
GV840.S5B66 1986 797.3'5 85-23062
ISBN 0-8225-1140-1 (lib. bdg.)

Manufactured in the United States of America

International Standard Book Number: ~~0-8225-1146-0~~
Library of Congress Catalog Card Number: 85-23792

1 2 3 4 5 6 7 8 9 10 95 94 93 92 91 90 89 88 87 86

Hi, I'm Anne Marie. In the summer, I often visit my grandparents who live on Prior Lake. This summer, I learned to water ski with my friend Wendy. We discovered that waterskiing is both fun and challenging. I love skimming over the water and just enjoying the ride, but I know that more advanced skiers also enjoy improving their skills and their endurance.

A lot of equipment is needed for waterskiing. First, you need a ski boat. The best boat for a young beginner has at least a 25-**horsepower** motor. The more horsepower a motor has, the more powerful it is, and the more weight the boat can pull.

The front passenger seat of a ski boat should face the back of the boat or swivel enough to face the back. The person sitting there is called the **observer** and will be watching the skier for the driver.

We also learned that a good ski boat must have a towing hitch, either a **pylon** or a **towbar**. The hitch is shaped like a small hoop or triangle, and the rope that tows the skier is tied here.

A pylon is used with inboard motorboats and is located in the center of the boat. A towbar, used with outboards, should be positioned in the middle of the back end of the boat. If the rope were attached to a hitch on one side of the boat instead of in the middle, the skier could capsize the boat when he or she skied to that side.

To keep the skier well away from the boat's motor, the tow rope should be 75 feet long. It should be made of a material that floats and should have a **breaking strength** of 1,500 pounds. The breaking strength is how much weight it takes to break the rope.

Our instructor's name was Steve. He is a neighbor of my grandparents, and he recently opened a ski school on Prior Lake. For our first lesson, Steve, Wendy, and I

met on the dock and looked at the water-skiing equipment. We learned that children's skis, called **junior skis**, are 55 inches long, 6 inches wide, and ½ inch thick. Junior skis are made of wood, and their tips curve upward so they can go over the water more easily. Each ski has a **foot binder** on top in the middle of the ski and a small **fin** on the underside at the back.

The foot binder holds the skier's foot on the ski. Foot binders, also called "bindings," are made of a soft gum rubber or a firmer molded rubber. Bindings must be easy to adjust, and they should lock firmly in place and not slip. No part of the binder should have sharp pieces sticking out, or bad cuts could result. To get a good fit when trying on the binders, always wet your feet and

the binders, too. If you don't, the binders will seem loose when they get wet later. Also, avoid letting the skis touch any sand. Sand will scratch the skis' surface and ruin their finish.

The fin is a small blade made of either metal or plastic that is located at the back of the ski on the lower side. Fins help to steer the skis better in the water.

An extremely important piece of waterskiing equipment is the **flotation device**, preferably a ski vest. The vest is used by beginning skiers and by advanced skiers for trick skiing, slalom skiing, and high-speed racing. A vest gives much more protection than a ski belt during hard spills,

and it should fit snug enough so that it won't slip off when you fall. Because a vest floats the skier higher in the water than a belt, it will hold a skier's head above water if the skier becomes hurt or unconscious. In addition to wearing a flotation device, a waterskier should be a fairly good swimmer because skiing is done in deep water.

After we had talked about the skier's equipment and tried it on, Steve told us that we had to learn several safety rules before we could ski. First, we should always be very familiar with the area where we were going to ski. Both the driver and the skier should know if there are any under-

water obstacles such as tree branches or rocks or any strong currents. Steve said that even when starting or landing, we should *always* ski in water more than five feet deep. He said that obstacles are much more common near the shore and that suddenly hitting something when going so fast could cause a serious injury.

Steve also told us to avoid skiing behind an unfamiliar boat or with an unfamiliar driver. Waterskiing requires a lot of teamwork between the driver and the skier, and getting used to the way a boat handles and a driver's towing style are both part of learning to be on the team.

For safe skiing, the driver and the skier need to know what to expect from each other. Before each ski session, tell your driver where you want to ski, how fast you want to go, and how long you want to stay out.

Never ski without an observer in the boat. This person will watch the skier and tell the driver if the skier falls or is signaling to change speed, to turn, or to land. A good observer keeps a careful watch on the skier and *does not* sightsee.

FASTER

SLOWER

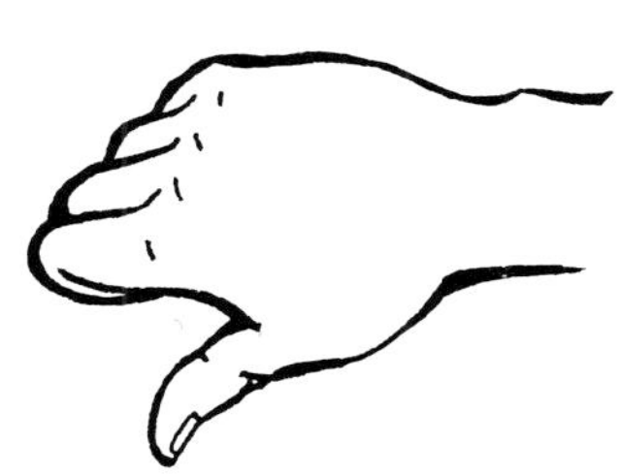

SPEED O.K.

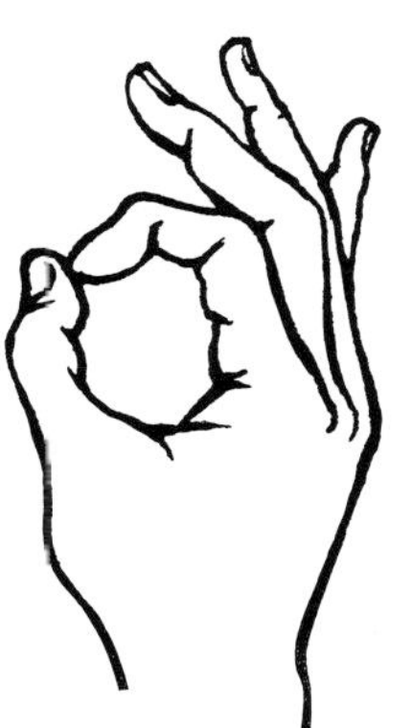

A skier "talks" to the observer by using **hand signals**. Steve showed us some of the most often used signals. "Thumbs up" means to go faster, and "thumbs down" means to go slower. A small "O" made with the thumb and the index finger means the speed of the boat is just right. Signal the driver to turn by making a circular motion with the index finger in the direction that you want to turn. When you want to stop, put your hand flat, palm down, in front of your throat.

TURN

I'M O.K.

PICK ME UP or **WATCH OUT—FALLEN SKIER**

If you fall and you're O.K., raise your arms overhead and join your hands. If you don't use this signal after falling, the driver will assume you're hurt and in need of assistance. If you fall and want to be picked up, hold one ski halfway out of the water. This signal also helps other boaters see you and avoid coming too close to you. The last signal is easy! If you want to ski back to the dock, just pat the top of your head.

BACK TO DOCK

The final safety rule we learned was that a skier should never be brought in closer than 150 feet to the shore, dock, or other boaters. If you come closer, your momentum might cause you to collide with something and hurt yourself.

Our next lesson was again on the dock at the edge of the lake. Steve said we should first practice getting up on our skis while out of the water. We wet our feet and the bindings so the bindings would slide on easily, and we could get a proper fit. Then Steve told us to sit back on the skis. Knees are bent up to the chest, arms and elbows are straight, and the head is up. We held the handle of the rope in both hands with our fingers down and our knuckles up. This hold is called the **grip**.

Steve picked up the free end of the rope so that he could act as the power of the

boat. Then, while I held on to the handle, he began to give a strong, steady pull on the rope. He told us that instead of trying to raise ourselves up with our arms and legs, we would be letting the pull of the boat bring us up almost to a stand. To do this, our arms should be straight out in front. Twisting our hands out and downward on the handle helped to keep our arms and elbows locked in a straight line. The head should always be up and the body weight should be directly over the skis. Once we are up, our knees should be slightly bent. We practiced this several times on the dock.

At the next lesson, we were ready to try getting up in the water. We put on our skis and slid into the lake. Steve had us move several feet away from the dock so we would not hit it if we fell.

Steve handed me the rope and told me to place the line between my skis. As the boat moved off and the slack went out of

the rope, I got crouched over the skis in the beginning position. The skis were to be angling toward the boat with their tips out of the water. When I was ready, Steve said to yell, "Hit it!" to the driver. Then he told me to concentrate on what I had learned in dry practice and to let the boat do the work of pulling me up.

The first time I tried to stand, I fell flat on my face! Steve said I had straightened my legs too soon, and the boat pulled me over.

Wendy fell backwards on her first try. Steve said her fall was caused by bending her elbows and pulling in on the rope as she came up out of the water. He also said that almost all beginners fall when they are first learning to ski. He told us that if we fell four times in a row, we should take a long rest. More tries would only make us too tired.

Both of us were lucky. We each got up on the third try, and the driver took each of us for a short ride on the lake. It felt like flying!

At our next lesson, Steve showed us how to put our skis on in deep water if we fell during a ride. First, grip the ski with one hand in the center near the binding. Then, with the other hand, hold the heel piece to one side. Put your foot into the front part of the binder and snap the heel piece on. Then put the second ski on in the same way. If you lose your balance, stay calm and don't struggle. Let your skis and rope float to the surface and then start again, slowly. When the skis are on, get in the starting position.

Next, Steve taught us how to turn. A beginner should turn by shifting his or her weight in the direction of the turn. That is, if you want to turn left, shift your weight to your left ski and lean a little in that direction. For faster turns, more advanced skiers dig into the water with the edge of the ski as they lean in the direction of the turn.

When we felt sure of our turns, Steve taught us how to cross the **wake**. The wake is the series of waves the boat leaves behind as it goes through the water. One wake fans out from each side of the boat, and together they make a V-shape. Steve said we should cross a wake as quickly as possible with our skis held fairly close together and parallel to each other. He said the

path of our skis should be as near to a right angle to the wake as possible and that we should always try to cross the wake with both skis at the same time. If you use only one ski at a time, the waves will sink the back ski, and you will fall. When crossing the wake, remember to bend your knees a bit more than usual to help absorb the shock of the larger waves.

It's not easy to ski across the rough water of the boat's wake! It took many spills and lots of practice for both of us before we felt sure of ourselves crossing the wake.

Steve said it was very important for a beginning waterskier to know how to do a good **landing**. A landing is a way for a skier to get back to shore when ready to take a break or stop skiing. The boat driver can get the skier near to the dock or the shore, but the skier must know the right way to let go of the ski rope.

Steve told us that it is best for the landing skier to stay right behind the boat between the wakes. As you approach the landing area, toss the handle of the rope to the side away from the shore. Glide toward the shore at an angle and, as you begin to slow, go into a crouch position as if you wanted to sit on the water.

Steve cautioned us to avoid heading directly for the shore. If you misjudge your speed or distance, you could hit the shore and have a bad fall. He said we should always be certain to land away from dangerous objects such as other boats, docks, or anything sticking out of the water. If you do see something in your path after you've let go of the rope, sit down in the water quickly. This will slow you down fast.

After we had practiced getting up, turning, crossing the wakes, and landing many times, Steve said the next step would be to learn about **slalom skiing**. Slalom skiing means skiing with only one ski. A special fiberglass slalom ski has larger fins than those on junior skis. Since both feet are on one ski, the extra control of the larger fin is needed.

The slalom ski has regular bindings for one foot in front and a toe piece for the other foot in back. The slalom ski is narrower than a junior ski and is made specially for turning.

As Steve told us more about slaloming, we watched Joey, one of the more advanced students in Steve's Ski School. Slalom skiing is often learned by starting with two skis and then dropping one. Usually a slalom ski is worn on the stronger leg and a junior ski on the other leg. In slalom skiing, the grip changes and the palm is up for one hand and down for the other. Since higher speeds are used for slaloming, gloves are often worn for a better grip and to avoid blisters.

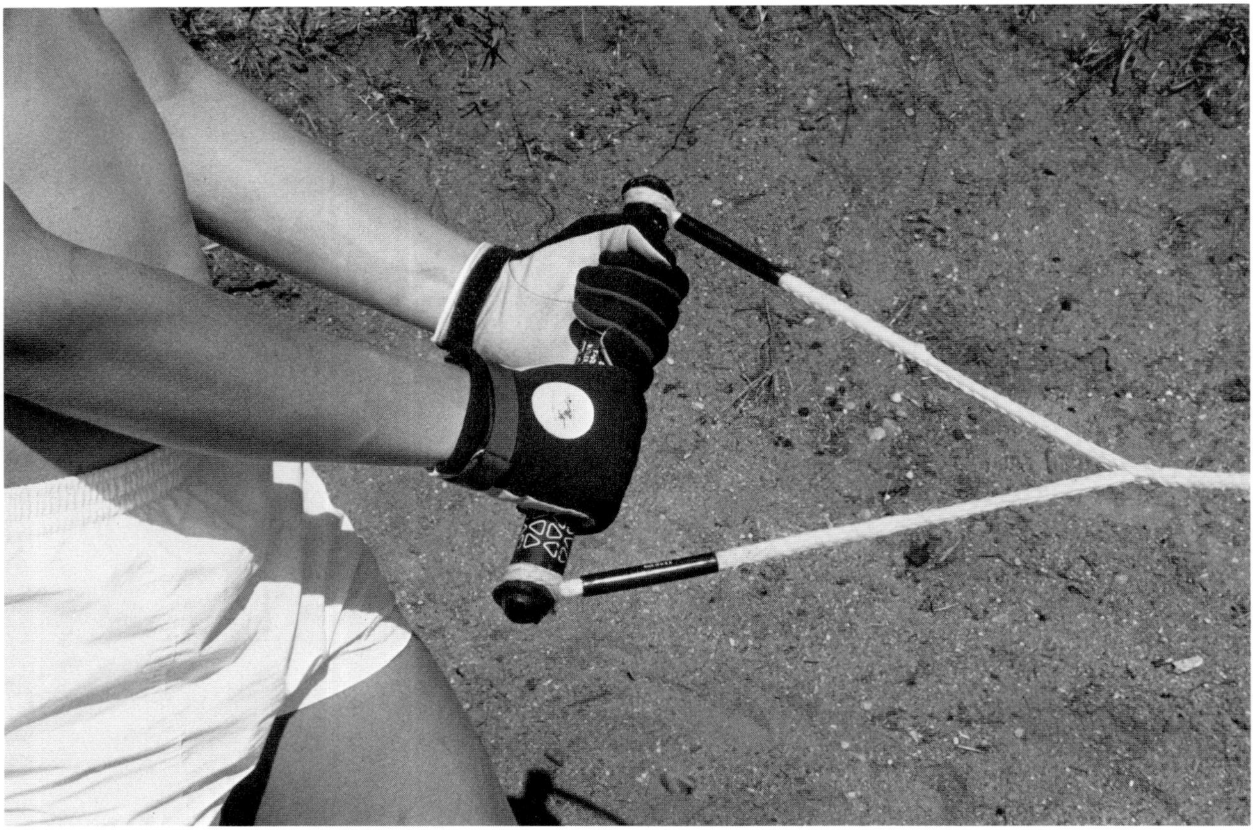

Joey first demonstrated slalom skiing on the dock. He raised his heel out of the binding on the junior ski and then slid his foot out of the binding. (The junior ski will be swept away by the water and picked up later.) Concentrating on keeping his balance, Joey slowly placed his free foot on the back of the slalom ski. When he was comfortable with all of his weight over one ski, he edged his back foot into the toe piece.

Later, as we watched Joey slalom in water, Steve told us it was very important to keep the rear heel flat on the ski. Some skiers let their back heel raise up, but this gives them less control of the slalom ski.

Then Wendy and I rode in the boat while Steve slalomed at high speeds around **buoys**, or floats, that mark a special course in the water. A regulation slalom course is 285 yards long by 25 yards wide with six turning buoys. Because slalom turns are both sharp and fast, the spray of water is often spectacular.

At another lesson, Steve had Wendy and I watch some of his younger beginning students as they skied. Joey helped a few of them remain steady while they prepared to get up. One little boy who skied really well was only eight years old. It was helpful to watch other beginners and to think again about the techniques for good skiing that Steve wanted us to remember.

Waterskiing is truly a family sport. After I had gained enough strength and experience, Steve suggested we try a "three-generation" pull. With four ropes tied to the pylon at once, Steve skied alongside my mom, my grandmother, and me!

One day after our lesson, we watched Steve practice **barefoot skiing**. Skiing without skis takes a lot of strength because it must be done at extremely fast speeds. Steve said it helps to imagine you're trying to stop the boat by leaning back on the heels of your feet. The falls are usually hard, but once you've skied barefoot, you know you've accomplished quite a feat.

Later, using a shorter, wider, and more rounded ski with no fin, Steve did some **trick skiing** for us. Some of his stunts were simply amazing!

Wendy and I practiced our skiing almost every day. Toward the end of the summer, my grandparents had a special surprise for us. We all went to a real waterski show! The show was produced by a group of people who had spent a lot of time practicing waterskiing routines together.

My favorite part of the show was the **jump skiing**. The jump, located in deep water, is a wooden ramp with water streaming down its incline. The skier skis up the slope and then flies off the high end, about four to six feet above the surface of the water. It takes a lot of skill to do jumps well.

Wendy liked **kite skiing** the best. In kite skiing, the skier starts out as usual but then becomes airborne as the boat increases speed. Because it is more risky than other types of skiing, kite skiing should be attempted only by very excellent skiers and drivers.

My mom liked the **mixed doubles skiing**, which is done by a man and a woman. In one trick, the couple started out skiing side by side. Then the woman dropped her skis as she climbed onto the man's shoulders. The man kept skiing and held her high while she posed in several arched positions. It will be a long time before Wendy and I can try that!

The show ended with a terrific three-high **pyramid**. All eight skiers, including the two flag carriers, made it back to the shore without a fall.

As we left the show, I thought about how exciting it is to fly over the water on a pair of skis. Wendy and I couldn't wait to take more lessons and to practice our skills. Maybe someday we'll be in a show, too. We think waterskiing is the most thrilling sport there is!

WATERSKIING Words

BARefoot SKIING: Skiing without skis

BINDERS (or BINDINGS): The rubber "shoe" on the top of the ski

BREAKING STRENGTH: The amount of weight it takes to break a rope

BUOY: A floating object, often red in color, anchored in the water and used to mark turns or warn of shallow water

FIN: A metal piece added to the back of a ski to help the skier steer

FLOTATION DEVICE: A vest or belt that keeps the fallen skier from sinking

GRIP: How the hands are placed on the towbar

HAND SIGNALS: Motions used by the skier to give instructions to the observer

HORSEPOWER: The measure of how powerful a motor is

JUMP SKIING: Skiing up a triangular wooden ramp and flying off the high end

JUNIOR SKIS: Children's wooden skis, smaller than adult skis, with tips that curve upward

KITE SKIING: Skiing while holding on to a bar underneath a kite and becoming airborne as the boat goes faster

LANDING: Getting rid of the ski rope when ready to stop skiing

MIXED DOUBLES SKIING: A man and a woman skiing together behind the same boat

OBSERVER: The boat passenger who faces the back of the boat to watch the skier for the driver

PYLON: A metal hoop in the center of an inboard motorboat used as a hitch for the ski rope

SLALOM SKIING: Skiing with only one ski for both feet

TOWBAR: The hoop located high on the back and middle of an outboard motorboat used as a hitch for the ski rope

TRICK SKIING: A series of stunts done with a short, rounded ski

WAKE: The two V-shaped waves made by a boat passing through the water

For information about a ski club in your area, contact:

American Water Ski Association (AWSA)
P.O. Box 191
Winter Haven, FL 33880

AWSA is the governing body for sanctioned waterski tournaments in the United States.

ABOUT THE AUTHOR

CAROLE S. BRIGGS enjoys water sports of all kinds and has spent summers SCUBA diving in Tahiti and on Australia's Great Barrier Reef. She has written several related books, including SKIN DIVING IS FOR ME, DIVING IS FOR ME, and SPORT DIVING. A graduate of the University of Wisconsin, Carole lives in Madison, Wisconsin, with her husband and two young sons.

ABOUT THE PHOTOGRAPHERS

BOB AND DIANE WOLFE have a freelance photography business in Minneapolis, Minnesota. Bob studied photography at the Minneapolis College of Art and Design and was senior medical photographer at the University of Minnesota. Diane works as a nursing instructor in St. Paul, Minnesota, and, in addition to her interest in photography, is an accomplished potter.